Marion H. Bowman

Copyright © 2015

# Table of Contents

# Chapter 1

## Introduction:

Stress, depression and anxiety are very common phenomena in this present age. The causes of these can be anything from non-satisfying job, broken marriages and relationships, inability to meet financial needs, ill health, wars, etc. There is always one challenge or the other will constantly put people under pressure and drive away confidence and calmness from them. Inner peace seems to have eluded many people and so the quest for these inner peace and joy is unavoidable.

So many forms of activities and exercises have been proffered as the panacea for freedom from these worries and anxieties. One of the most prominent and effective activity that is making waves globally is Zentangle. Practiced by many people all over the world, this special form of art has recorded many testimonies from its users, having brought them relief and the peace and serenity which they so much desire. Solutions to even the hardest problems and unlimited creativity which seemed not to be there previously, have been unleashed by this art.

Zentangle is an art which anyone who desire to excel, achieve goals and enjoy the real essence of life should practice.

In this write-up, I will tell you everything that you need to know about this great art, why more and more people are engaging it, why you should join and how you can start. Welcome to the free world of ZENTANGLE.

# WHAT IS ZENTANGLE?

Zentangle is an art that is widely spreading across the world, with hundreds of thousands of people actively engaging in it. With just a pen and a plain paper, people are busy drawing out patterns that only make sense at the end and are achieving a lot of personal benefits through it. What is this zentangle that is causing this wave around the world?

Zentangle is a form of art work made from drawing a repetitive pattern on a square tile with 3.5inch diameter. It is drawn on a white sheet with a black ink. This new form of art is not just an ordinary art; it is a special one that brings a feeling of self-worth, freedom from worry and anxiety and a total serenity to your life. Zentangle tries to give you a new perspective to life and helps you enjoy your life better.

In zentangle, there is no right or wrong drawing; everything is right and so is especially good for beginners in art who shy away from making mistakes when drawing. Mistakes in zentangle are converted by the one drawing the patterns, into something totally different and unique. This tries to teach you something about life: you can make mistakes, but you should rather than go backwards trying to erase it, move forward and try to convert the mistake into something valuable in your life.

When drawing zentangle, you do not need to have a particular image or artwork in mind which you intend drawing. You have to start it with an empty mind and allow your mind control your hand on what to do. Since you are not supposed to have anything in mind to achieve while drawing a zentangle, the end result is always a unique and beautiful work of art that gives an inner joy to the artist.

Those who draw zentangles are called zentanglers while the art of drawing it is called tangling.

If you have never practiced zentangle, it makes a lot of sense to try it. The experience is a rewarding as you would learn later from this writing.

# Chapter 2

## Zentangle and Other forms of Arts:
## WHY IS ZENTANGLE DIFFERENT FROM OTHER FORMS OF ART?

Many people confuse zentangle with other forms of art. There is a very wide difference between it and other forms of art. Unlike other forms of art, zentangle is a form of meditation for people that engage in it. The final result of a zentangle drawing is always beautiful and satisfying to the person drawing it. The other things that differentiate zentangle from other forms of art include:

- If you are an artist and you set out to draw, you will have particular image you want to draw, or a particular message you wish to convey in your art work. This will guide your drawing and you will know when you actually achieved it.

  This is not so with zentangle. You do not set out to draw a particular image in zentangle. This means that when starting out to draw a zentangle, you have no definite result in mind that you wish to achieve. You just allow your mind to flow and to control your hands. You should let the pattern you are drawing reveal itself as you draw. Whatever is formed at the end is always awesome and attractive.

- An artist can make mistakes when drawing. That is why he needs to keep an eraser beside him as he does his work. But it is not so with zentangles as there are no mistakes when drawing. Every mistake is used as a foundation to start a new pattern, which will result in an unanticipated pattern. The feeling that you are able to create something beautiful out of your mistake gives a feeling of fulfillment.

- For an artist to draw something amazing, he needs a lot of tools to work with: pen, pencils, colors, eraser and even computer. It is not so with zentangle. Zentangle requires no technology or special tools for it to be used. With pen and paper, you are good to go in drawing your beautiful zentangle.
- It requires total focus. It is not an art you can do when you are finding it difficult to concentrate, just like a doodle, which is drawn when you lack concentration, for example when making a phone call or when in a lecture room. It requires an undivided attention from you. Attention and focus is a very important form of this art.
- It is practiced in a quiet place. Since it does not require any form of distraction, a quiet place is ideal for drawing a zentangle, so that total concentration can be achieved.
- Perhaps the most important point that distinguishes zentangle from other forms of art is its supernatural effect. Zentangle drawings leads you into deep mediations during which you are able to gain a feeling of freedom for all your worries, serenity and joy in your soul and even healing from sickness that comes with the state of the mind.

# Chapter 3

## Who is Behind Zentangle?

Zentangle was founded by two couples in a hamlet at Whitinsville, central Massachusetts, Maria Thomas and Rick Roberts in 2003. Maria was an experienced calligrapher and Robert was formerly a monk in India.

One day, Maria was at work on an illuminated letter inside her studio. She was so engrossed in the beautiful pattern she was designing around the letter, that she did not even notice when her husband entered the studio. Her husband stood there observing her for some time. He knew she was already out of the physical and so interrupted her. She jerked and came back to life like someone waking up from a short nap.

She was so excited about the feelings she felt inside during the period; feelings of being set free from worries, troubles and any other thing that steals the concentration or peace of mind away. She immediately shared the experience with her husband. Having been a monk previously, Robert instantly understood that his wife has just come out of a meditation session.

They practiced this new found way of meditation through art over and over again and saw that it felt good and so felt compelled to show this beautiful system of combining art and meditation to the world. Robert called himself the Zen while Maria called herself the Tangle and that was how the name Zentangle came to be.

Working together on the project of showcasing this system to the world, they transformed Zentangle into what it is today: a work of art with meditative powers to help anyone who so wishes, to attain fulfillment, inner peace and a sense of belonging. The couples believe that if you can write, you can be able to zentangle. Their driving force has been their belief that every living being has the gift of art within him which can only be expressed when the person can develop the confidence to try it out. Since zentangle has no expected end result, you can draw any pattern they way your mind moves you to and still end up creating something that is extremely beautiful.

Hundreds of thousands of people around the world has given great testimonies about the meditative and therapeutic effects of zentangle in their lives. The couples taught people about using the art to experience good feelings about themselves, but the results that their students are receiving from it far exceeds what the couples thought was the only resultant effect of the art.

Recently, the couple published their first book titled: "The Book of Zentangle". Continuously, they have been working in this area to improve themselves and so many others who practice the art. This is what Robert had to say about it: "Just as Maria speaks of discovering new colors, I imagine developing new symbolic languages unconstrained by the too-tight shoes of words and learned presumptions of body/mind splits and classical world views."

# Chapter 4

## What can you learn from Zentangle?

Zentangle is an art, but not just an ordinary art. Practicing it comes with so many benefits physically, spiritually and emotionally. Take a look at some of the benefits of practicing zentangle:

- As zentangle requires great focus to produce a great result, it helps you improve your hand to eye coordination. In addition you will discover that your dexterity in committing what is in your mind to paper will also be greatly boosted.

- Many of life's challenges can be solved through zentangle drawing. During your drawing, your focus and creativity is increased and so the answers to the many questions and challenges you are facing will surface.

- When you are stressed up after the day's activities, engaging in zentangle drawings can be a great way to free yourself of the stress, by taking your mind of it and focusing it on your drawing. This will bring great calm and inner peace to you.

- Zentangle can help boost your self-esteem. When you are able to create a great art design from your zentangle, there is a great feeling of accomplishment and pride you get within you which ultimately boosts your self-esteem.

- Your natural skills and creativity can be greatly improved through zentangle. Since there is no right or wrong way to tangle, you are unlimitedly free to explore your natural creativity the way you like. At the end, you discover a part of you which you previously never knew of; your creativity in art.

- Zentangle can be a great way to relieve you of anger. So those who are easily provoked or find themselves staying angry for a prolonged period can find help through zentangle. It will relax your mind, making it drift from whatever is causing you anger, to feelings of joy and peace within.

- You can enjoy a good night's sleep with the help of zentangle. When you are able to free yourself from the cares and worries of life through zentangle, then you discover that you will be able to sleep better. Since good sleep can boost your immune system, zentangle will also indirectly boost your immunity through helping you sleep well.

- The art of zentangle can be a source of inspiration to you. To be able to draw beautiful art works, you will get inspiration from within you and from your environment. So constant practice of zentangle will lead you to easily draw inspiration from uncommon places to be able to produce great works.

- The Zentangle slogan is: "Anything is possible; one at a time". Your drawing which you cannot tell how you started can produce a great and beautiful work of art which can turn out to inspire others and give you recognition.

- There have also been reports about the therapeutic effect of zentangle from its users all over the world.

Research shows that many of the sickness we suffer come from the state of our mind. Since zentangle helps rid your mind of all ill feelings, health and serenity can be restored to you through the practice of zentangle.

- Zentangle can be done individually, producing great works. There are also possibilities of drawing zentangle as a group, forming a perfect group activity that can foster team building.

- Finally, practicing zentangle teaches you among other things, how to concentrate. So whether you are in class or reading, if you are an addicted user of zentangle, your ability to focus and concentrate is greatly sharpened, leading you to perform excellently in whatever you are doing.

Did you ever think zentangle could help you achieve all these? I guess your answer is No! So I encourage you to try it. You will have your experiences to share.

# Chapter 5

## Interested in Zentangle! Let's Begin

Creating your own zentangle is very simple. Since there is
no right or wrong zentangle, you should not bother about
creating something so exquisite at first. So how do you go
about drawing your first zentangle?

First, you need to get the right materials. The materials you
need include a white art paper with a dimension of 3.5 X
3.5. This you will use as a foundation of your zentangles.
Using a colored paper is allowed, but it will not be
considered as a true zentangle going by the zentangle
method.

Secondly, you need to draw the border of the zentangle.
Using a pencil, make a dot in each corner of the paper, and
then connect the dots. Remember not to use a ruler in
connecting the dots. Sketch it near the edges of the paper
lightly. Don't be afraid of mistakes as you draw the lines.
Mistakes will actually make it look unique and original
when you are fully and finally done with the zentangle. It
is good you remember to sketch this borders and not to
press down the pencil as to form thick lines. The borders
should not be visible after you are done with the drawing.

Thirdly, draw a string inside the border using your pencil. A string according to the zentangle method will lend structure to your drawing and is usually a curved line or a squiggle. The contours of your strings will determine how your pattern will look. Remember that there is no right or wrong way to do this. So it should be sketchy, simple and abstract in form as it will form the basis for the different sections of your drawings. You should note that these strings are meant to serve as a guide for drawing your pattern, so don't make it thick. It should be sketchy.

To some, drawing these strings is difficult, but it should not be so for you. It should flow naturally. Whatever your hand is led to draw, just obey it; there is no right or wrong drawing, so just draw as it comes. Check online for ideas on creating strings. There are many string patterns online for you to get inspiration from.

Fourthly, you should start creating your tangle. By tangle, I mean drawing patterns along the string's contours. At this stage, you need to use your pen in drawing. Feel free to draw the patterns in whichever the feeling comes to you. Remember that there is no right or wrong way to draw your patterns. Just flow along with the inspiration. You can use pencil to shade some parts of the tangle so as to produce something very awesome.

You need to always keep in mind that there is nothing like mistakes in zentangle and so you don't need to wipe anything you feel was done in error. Rather, when you feel you have made a mistake, use it as a springboard to draw something new and beautiful.

Focus is also very essential. Keep your mind on the drawing till you are done with it. The real essence of zentangle is to rid your mind of all things that disturbs its peace. So don't drift into thoughts about your day or issues you have in any area of your life. Concentrate and keep your mind consistently on the drawing. This is the only way you can achieve the full benefits of zentangle as stated previously.

# Chapter 6

## From Where Can you draw Inspiration?

Possibly you are already addicted to zentangle, drawing lots and lots of similar pattern which may now be boring you, and having seen lots and lots of more beautiful zentangles that people have done either on the internet or around your neighborhood. How do you derive inspiration to draw better and more inspiring and scintillating zentangles? The answer is simple: "it is right where you are".

You will be surprised at the number of zentangle patterns you will see around you if you consciously observe. Look at your sink; the bubbles therein, your floor tiles, window blinds, roof tiles, bamboo furniture, fences, bricks. Carpets and wallpapers, bowl of beads viewed as circles, paving stones, potted plants, bookshelves with books in stacked in it, etc.

Another unlimited source of zentangle pattern is nature: branches of trees, grasses, leaves, flowers, beach, hills, birds flying in the sky and so on.

If you look, you will sure see patterns everywhere. To help you remember these patterns, you can take notes of beautiful patterns you see or capture them with a camera if you have one. This could just be your phone's camera. Another way to come up with a new pattern for your zentangle is by checking the previous patterns you have done, and seeing how you could come up with something different and unique from it.

# HOW TO BE BETTER AT ZENTANGLE

If you love zentangle, you would be amazed at the so many wonderful zentangles that others have created. It may sometimes intimidate you into thinking that you can never be as good as they are. The truth is that you can. How?

By constantly practicing.

It is as simple as that. The so many artists whom you admire their works did not get to that level on their first zentangle drawing. They may have had dozens if not scores of works they and probably you would not be proud of. So if you would want to get into their level, then you need to practice as constant as they do.

If you seriously want to become very good at zentangle and draw patterns that will catch the attention of anyone that comes around it, then you should get a journal with plain pages. Then try drawing one zentangle into it daily if you can. If you have a tight schedule such that you can't do it daily, then trying it once or thrice a week will do. You can also participate in many zentangle challenges out there; you can easily find one out there. If you have the knowledge, you can start blogging about your zentangle patterns, uploading it for others to see. Also you can follow great zentangle artist on social media or on their blogs so that you can always get challenging inspirations from them. Commenting on their patterns and asking them questions in a non-spamming manner will also connect you more to them and help you learn deeper.

Finally, discipline yourself enough to practice this and before you know it, you will become great at zentangle drawings.

## Chapter 7

### Drawing Simple Zentangle Patterns

Starting out in zentangle and producing a great masterpiece is always elusive. Most people do not know the pattern to come up with, so I decided to show you how to draw simple patterns in zentangle. As you are able to do this, you will easily progress into producing complex designs from your own creativity.

Here are ten simple zentangle patterns you can start with:

### ALPHABET ZENTANGLE

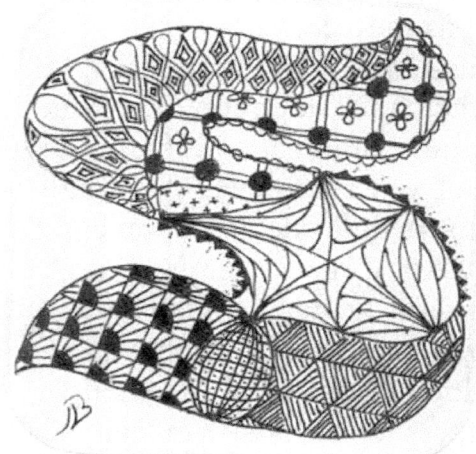

To draw and alphabet zentangle, follow the following procedures:

- First draw a block letter. This can be the first letter of a word or maybe the initials of your name
- Next, you have to draw sections within the letter and or sections around the border.
- Lastly, add a pattern into each section.

You can add more letters to it to form a word.

## DRAWING A HOLLIBAUGH

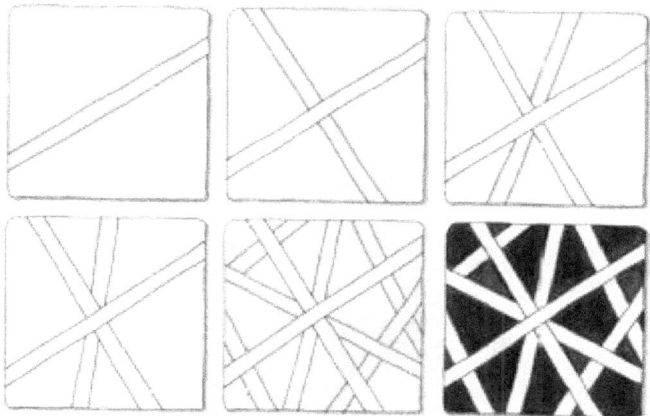

To draw a hollibaugh, follow these steps:

- First draw two parallel lines across a section.
- Secondly, you rotate the tile then draw another pair of lines making it look as if these new pair is under the first one.
- Thirdly, you should rotate the tile again and draw another pair of lines that looks as if it is under the first two.
- Fourthly, continuously keep rotating the tile and keep drawing new parallel line till the tile is full.
- Lastly, use your pen to add a black background to the tile if you so wish. This background should not interfere with the parallel lines you drew.

There you have hollibaugh.

## DRAWING A PRINTEMPS

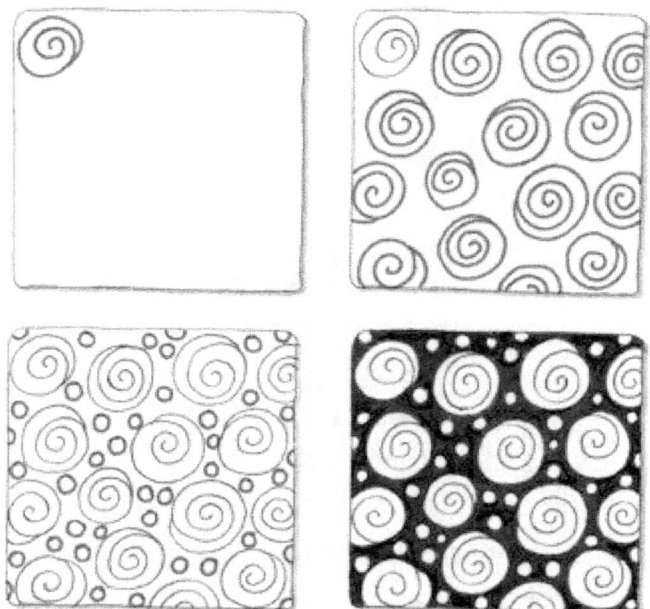

To draw a printemps, just follow these steps:

- First, you should draw a series of circles. These circles should vary in sizes starting from one end of the page and radiating outwards.
- The second step is to fill in each of the circles with spirals and semi-complete circles. See the picture above
- Lastly, you can choose to color the background with your pen. A dark background would be fine.

# DRAWING A GINGHAM

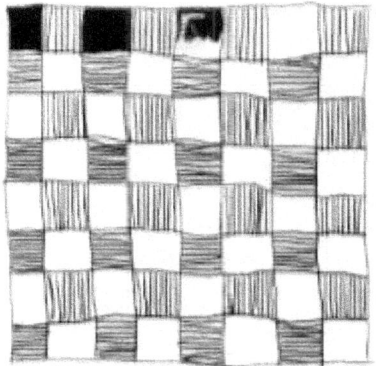

Follow these steps to draw gingham:

- First, you draw a basic outline. This outline can be perfectly straight or could be curvy. It all depends on you, though gingham normally has a straight outline. Nevertheless, do it like you would want since there is no right or wrong way zentangle.
- Secondly, fill in alternating squares with color using your pen
- In the spaces remaining, you should draw a series of line which could have same color with the filled squares or with different color.

# DRAWING AN ARC FLOWER

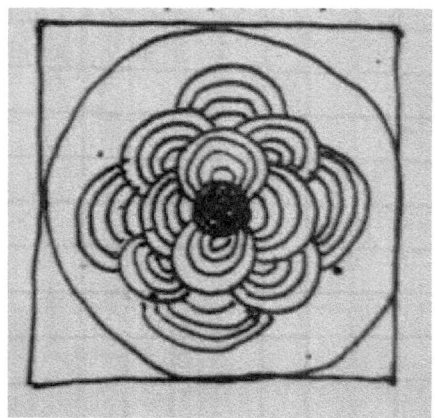

Following the following simple steps will lead you to drawing an arc flower:

- First, you should draw a big circle.
- Secondly, draw a smaller circle inside the big circle. When drawing this smaller circle, see if you can accurately make it to be in the center of the big center.
- Thirdly, draw four to five curved lines on the top and bottom sides of the small circle which is centered inside the big one. These curves should be radiating outwards as shown in the picture above.
- Fourthly, draw another four to five curves between the ones drawn in step three above. These new curves should also be radiating outwards. See the picture above to understand.
- Continue drawing new curves using these patterns described, until the edges of the curves reaches the edge of the bigger outer circle.

- You can decide to color the spaces remaining between the big circle and the curves as shown in the picture.

There you have it drawn: an arc flower.

## DRAWING A CRESCENT MOON

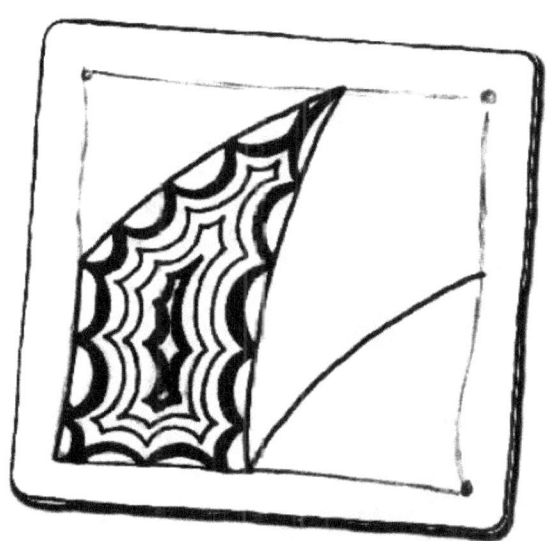

Following these simple steps will produce a beautiful crescent moon:

- First draw your borders and sections. You can borrow a leaf from the image above
- Next, draw curved humps along the inside edges of any section
- Next, draw a moon or arched shaped curves on each hum drawn above

- You then with your pen, color the moon-like shape drawn above with black
- Next, you should draw a curved line inside the moons. This line should be continuous without breakage.
- Finally, to fill the section, draw additional lines inside the section.

## DRAWING S STATIC

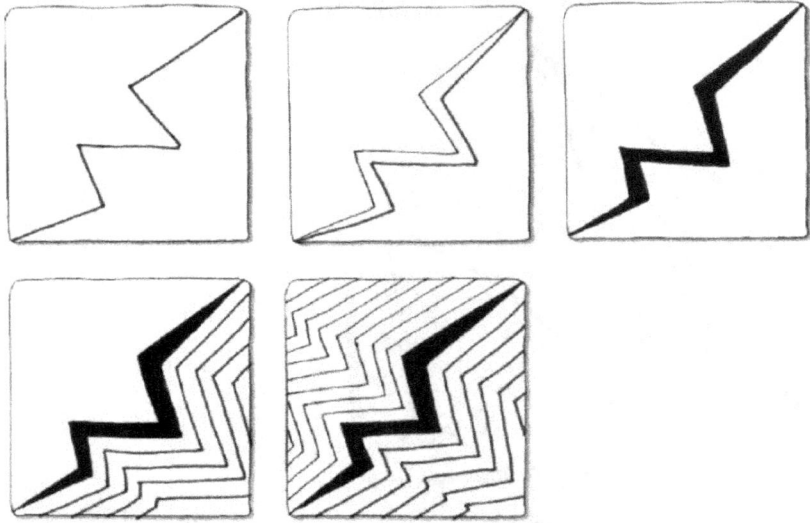

This is simple and can be drawn in these easy to follow steps:

- As usual, draw your borders and section.
- Next, you draw a zigzag line from one end of a section to the other end
- Next, draw another zigzag line that is parallel to the one you drew above. Ensure that at the ends of these zigzag lines, they both meet each other.

- Now, you should fill the zigzag shape with a black color
- On one side of the joined zigzag line, draw additional lines parallel to the zigzag. But this time, the lines shouldn't join themselves. Continue this till that side of the section is filled up
- When done with one side, turn to the other side of the section and draw similar parallel lines that don't touch themselves. Repeat this also till that part of the section is filled up.

Now you have a static zentangle.

## DRAWING A HAIRY ZENTANGLE

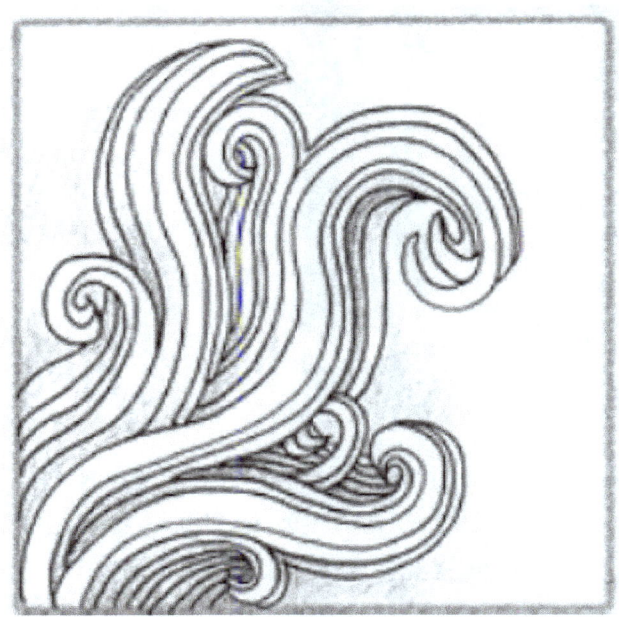

- First, draw your border

- Then draw some wavy lines pointing to different directions
- Add more lines beside the ones you drew in the step above.
- Continuously keep adding more lines till the whole page is filled.

**DRAWING THE EDDIES**

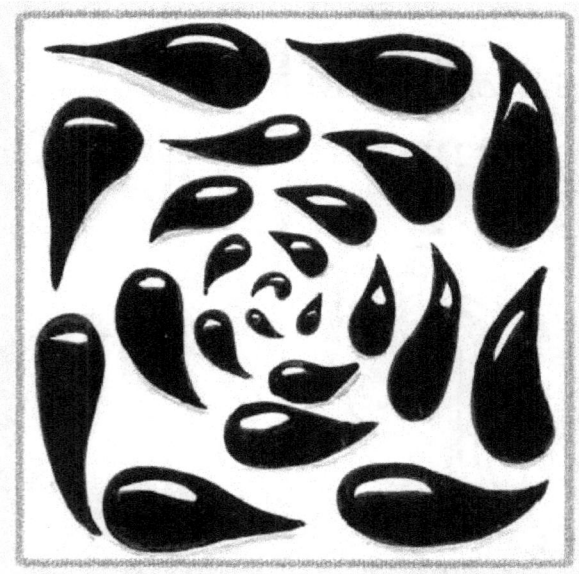

This you can easily achieve by following these steps:
- The first step after drawing your border is to draw many raindrop-shapes in a semi-circle manner

- Next, draw more raindrop shapes as above, but these ones should be smaller and should try to complete the semi-circle manner above, while spiraling inside.
- Continue drawing more of these smaller raindrop shapes, forming smaller and smaller circles, till they reach the center.
- To spice it up, draw small half-moon shapes at the end of the larger raindrops
- Finally, color all the raindrop shapes but not the half-moon shapes.

If you followed these steps, then your Eddie zentangle should have formed just like in the image above.

# DRAWING THE ONAMATO

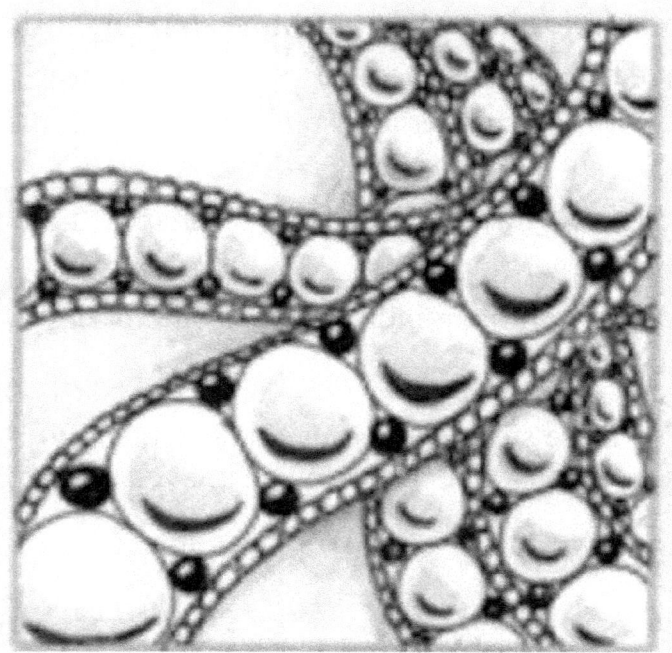

The last zentangle I do be showing you how to draw is the onamato. Drawing it can be achieved through the steps below:

- First draw your border. The borders should be a pattern of crossing lines as shown above.
- Next, draw large circles inside of the borders drawn above
- Now draw series of small circles within the space along each border
- Draw additional smaller circles at the corners where the bigger circles you first drew meet each other.
- To add flavor to the drawing, faintly shade the large circles and there you have it: an onamato

As you draw more and more simple zentangles, you will get better at it and produce great looking ones with time. Like I have written previously, you can draw inspiration from anywhere to produce yours. If you still need more samples of zentangles to inspire you, check the internet and you will lots and lots of other patterns to try.

Now this patterns which I just taught you how to draw is to help guide you in drawing your first zentangle. Try drawing yours from your initiative and see what you will come up with.

Remember you are not just drawing zentangles for the fun of it; it goes beyond it. If your drawing will not help you achieve perfect peace of mind and freedom from the cares and worries in your life, then you are merely doodling.

# Chapter 8

## Conclusion (Some common questions of a reader!)

Since the origin of zentangle, so many questions have risen about it from users and non-users. I will try and answer some of the most popular ones here:

**HOW DO I DERIVE THE MOST BENEFITS OUT OF MY ZENTANGLE DRAWING?**

To derive the most out of your zentangle drawings, you need to obey the basic rules involved with zentangles. These are:

- You must be totally focused and concentrated when drawing zentangles. Keep your whole mind off the happenings around you and focus completely in your drawing

- Do not erase the mistakes you feel you make while drawing zentangles. That is why you draw your borders and strings with a pencil, but tangle with a pen which cannot be easily erased. If you make mistake, continue on it and try to make something beautiful out of your supposed mistake. You will be surprised at the result you get afterwards.

- Apply the lessons you gain from it in your life. For example, you learn that you cannot erase your mistakes, but must build on it to make something successful and mind-blowing

- Don't start out with anything or shape in mind. Just keep your mind empty and let your hand do the work. Whatever or however your mind moves your hand to draw, just draw it. The outcome will amaze you.

- Continue practicing as you can only become better and better by practicing. This will not just boost your creativity in art, but will also increase the benefits you will derive from it.

## IS THERE A SIMILARITY BETWEEN ZENTANGLE AND YOGA?

Zentangle is a special art that leads you to meditate whereas Yoga is a physical stretching or exercise, which helps prepare your body for meditation. Whereas, the both might seem to have a common objective; to help you meditate right and achieve internal peace, the ways through which they achieve it is totally different.

## WHO CAN TEACH ME ZENTANGLE?

You can learn Zentangle by reading books and write-ups on the art just like this one, and practice on your own to perfect in it. But if you want to get even deeper into the art, learning the underlying philosophies of the art, then you need to look for a Zentangle class in your area to join. The zentangle classes are anchored by Certified Zentangle Teachers. You will learn a lot more from these teachers than you will learn by watching zentangle videos or reading zentangle books.

# HOW CAN I BECOME A ZENTANGLE TEACHER?

For you to become a Certified Zentangle Teacher (CZT), you must have been trained personally by the founders of Zentangle; Maria Thomas and Rick Roberts, at the Providence Rhode Island. People all over the world travel there yearly to learn directly from the founders and get certified. To become a CZT, go to the Zentangle website and apply. All the information you need for your registration is there.

# CONCLUSION

Zentangle can be practiced by anybody, both old and young and they will all derive the powerful benefits attached to entangle. It has real life applications that will make you make the most out of life. For example, zentangle can help young students to learn and understand better through its teachings on focus and concentration. If the students learn and understand better, then they will come out with better grades. For the older people who are more prone to worries and challenges in the family, workplace or in their relationship with people, zentangle will help them sort out those issues by creating peace within them. The best decisions and answers to challenges and problems are best gotten during time of perfect internal peace and this is what zentangle can guarantee those who practice it.

Perhaps the most interesting part of zentangle is that you can easily get started. You don't need special skills or special equipment. All you need is your pen and plain paper and you are ready to tangle and enjoy the inherent sweet experiences associated with it. Just a little guidance such as those explained in this write-up can help you to create your first tangle.

So what are you waiting for? Join the hundreds of thousands of people around the world to tangle so you can enjoy a lasting peace and longevity. Your own experience will surely inspire many others to spread the message about zentangle. So start creating your first zentangle, not later, but NOW!

Welcome to the world of ZENTANGLE!

www.ingramcontent.com/pod-product-compliance
Lightning Source LLC
Chambersburg PA
CBHW070755180526
45168CB00004B/1618